THE WISDOM OF BEING HUMAN

Jean Lanier

With the compliments
of the author and the publisher.
This donation was made possible by
a grant from Mr. Laurance S. Rockefeller.

THE WISDOM OF BEING HUMAN

Jean Lanier

With Illustrations by Marion Weber

Integral Publishing
Lower Lake, California

Copyright © 1989 Jean Lanier
Illustrations, copyright © 1989 Marion Weber
All rights reserved.

First edition, 1989

Printed in the United States

Integral Publishing
P.O. Box 1030
Lower Lake, CA 95457

The art on the cover is a photographic reproduction of the marble sculpture "The Kiss" by Santa Barbara artist Dean Mars. Grateful acknowledgment is made to him for permission to use this image.

Cover design by Richard Stodart, San Francisco

For Katherine

Library of Congress Catalog Card Number 89-080345

Library of Congress Cataloging-in-Publication Data
Lanier, Jean, 1918-
  The wisdom of being human / Jean Lanier; with illustrations by Marion Weber. — 1st ed.
      p. cm.
    ISBN 0-941255-40-9 : $13.95. — ISBN 0-941255-39-5 (pbk.) : $7.95
    1. Meditations. I. Title.
BV48322.L318 1989
242—dc20
                                                          89-80345
                                                              CIP

92 91 90 89
10 9 8 7 6 5 4 3 2 1

Contents

Foreword	6
Author's Preface	8
The Evolution of Eve	11
The Awakening of Adam	69
The Liberation of Isaac and Abraham	121
About the Author	151
About the Artist	151

Foreword
by David F. K. Steindl-Rast

A sentence that is brief yet clear, sparkles. Jean Lanier's writing has that sparkle. But let's not confuse sparkle with glitter. Have you ever noticed that those two differ as diamonds differ from tinsel? Glitter plays on the surface; it dazzles us and makes us dizzy. Sparkle gives us a sober delight; it has depth.

The three aphoristic stories in *The Wisdom of Being Human* have depth. They have the fire of diamonds. Their brevity does not result from clipping, but from distillation. Their fire is the sparkle of precision. Theologically as well as psychologically, they are precise: no mean achievement. But Jean Lanier knows the limits of precision. She has the grace to celebrate, not to dissect.

Too often, those who speak of the Bible as revelation forget that it is from beginning to end a tale of relationships. When they try to present "revealed truth" apart from those human and divine relationships, they are leading us to a shelf of frozen produce instead of opening a garden gate. With sure instinct, Jean Lanier does the opposite: She zeroes in on relationship. That's why she can afford to be brief: the key word fits. With the precision of a master key the concept of relationship unlocks the whole garden.

And what a garden it is! There is more here than precision. The coldness we tend to associate with precision is overcome by human warmth. Jean Lanier has this warmth, because she gives herself to life, willingly, bravely, generously. Precision is bought at the price of hard work; human warmth is the fruit of suffering. The sparkle of it all is free gift, pure grace. This short book has grace. There is more compassionate wisdom in it than in many a ponderous tome. There is nothing ponderous about these pages, yet they are well worth pondering. I did ponder them with gratitude and am still thrilled.

Author's Preface

This book is about *I* and *you*. In my own life, I have observed that *I* seems to spend a great deal of time looking for, or at, *you*. Sometimes, sadly, *I* looks away.

On a larger scale, I think one could say that all of civilization is an expression of how *I* relate to *you*. When I and you are drawn together we have art, music, poetry, inspired religion, just government. When I turn away from you we have war, alienation, corruption, despair, chaos.

The *I* and *you* of this book are real people, in the sense that they are factual people with names and addresses. They are a lover, a parent, a child, myself. They are you and me. They are also real in the sense that they do *not* have names and addresses, but live in a realm where *I* and *you* are one reality.

This is the realm we explore in the great spiritual traditions. It is difficult to write about that realm with any degree of accuracy. Concepts and words can only point to it. We employ concepts and words in the hope that *I* and *you* will meet in the silence from which they emerge and to which they return. As languaged beings striving to speak honestly, we search for words to lead us to that
silence.

In that search, some of us are drawn to the wisdom

revealed in the study of theology or psychology, or both, as was my case. That wisdom helps us place our personal, time-bound stories in a larger human context. For me, the pondering required by these disciplines was liberating. It was through these ponderings that I came first to embrace my own story and then to release it from my possessive grasp. From these studies I learned that the word of God is spoken in human history and that reality is always *present* reality. I also watched the many you's of my life become, and remain, the ever-present You without whom I could not be *I.*

Acknowledgment

I wish to thank all those who have touched my life, for the truth is: I owe you my life.

THE EVOLUTION OF EVE

And the serpent inquired of Eve: "Did God really say that?"
Genesis (paraphrased)

Some day there will be girls and women whose name will no longer signify merely an opposite of the masculine, but something that makes one think of . . . life and existence.
Rainer Maria Rilke

Introduction

God didn't talk a lot, but Eve recalled that God had said *something*. At least, that is what Adam told her. Fortunately for the rest of humanity, Eve didn't pay too much attention. I don't think she really listened. We can be grateful for her distraction because without Eve's so-called disobedience, we might never have ventured forth into new experiences, much less reflected on them. We would be pretty boring.

The story that follows is about the experience of a broken heart. It begins before the heart breaks, passes through the rupture, and comes out on the other side where the healing begins.

A friend called this an "epigrammatic novel." Like the serpent, he posed an important question: "Why do you write in so brief a manner?" It was like this. When I was in seminary I had to write a dissertation that was meant to crown my years of study and demonstrate that I had a theological perspective on things. My work had the proper number of pages, footnotes, quotations, references, and a weighty title, best lost in the archives. It satisfied my professors, but it didn't satisfy Eve. She wanted me to tell it how it really is.

The Beginning

I am called Eve. There was a time when I was a part of you. I had no knowledge, then, of being different from you. I thought I was you. We were . . . each other. We had no history and no death. We were endless.

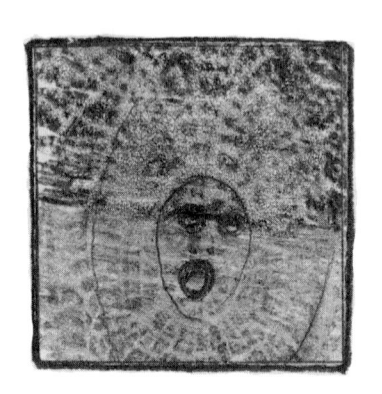

Temptation

Temptation

I wanted to make our happiness secure by giving it a name. But what was its name?

Desire

I became preoccupied with the need to know the answer to my question.

Punishment

The Fall

I didn't hear you when you spoke to me. I was distracted. I had discovered the answer to my question: It was *love*. I *loved* you.

Punishment

You have left me. Why?

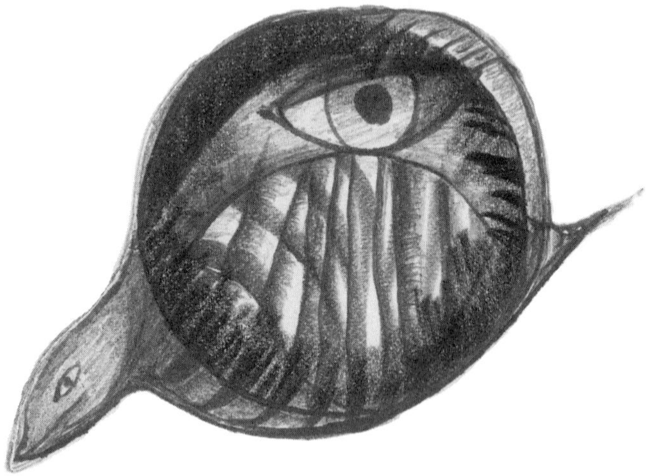

Expulsion from the Garden

Where are you? Without you I am afraid and want to die, but I am more afraid of death. I am becoming a burden to myself. I work but there is no joy in it. I am sick unto death of myself, and yet I don't know who I am.

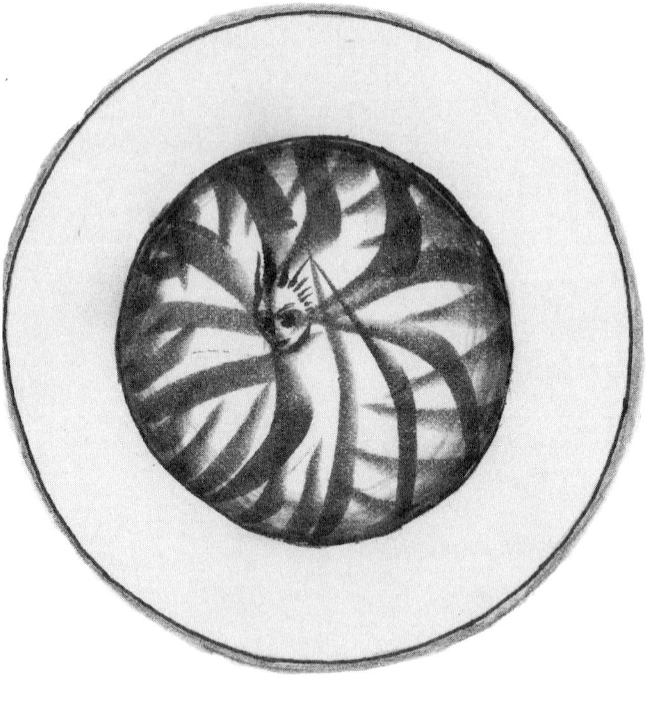

Cain and Abel

I have found a way to be rid of myself, by getting rid of others. I shut them out because it is too painful for me to listen to them. I hate them, which is my way of hating you. But I feel more alone than ever, and I live as a prisoner in myself.

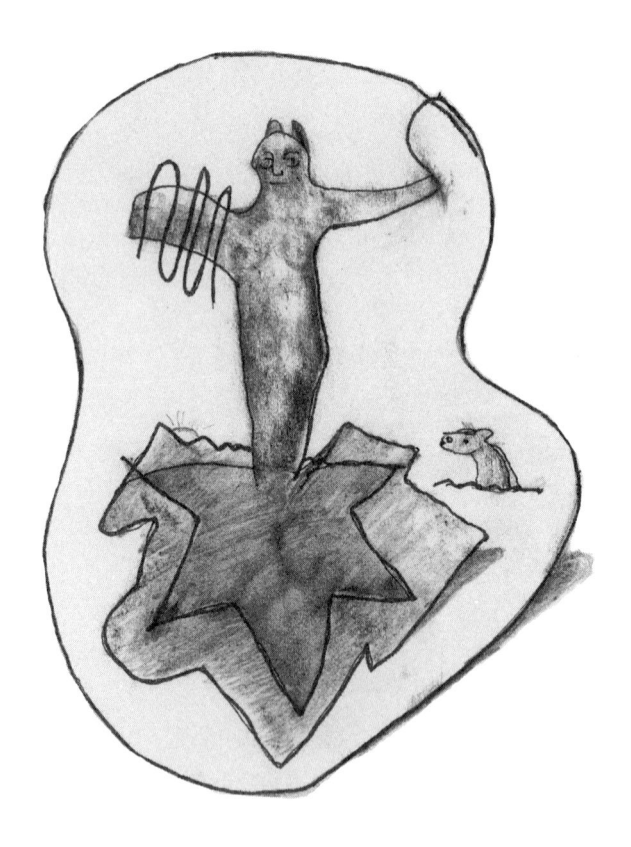

Evil

Idolatry

I worship you. Can't you see that you are everything to me? Come back to me, I will prostrate myself before you.

Evil

I have found a way out. If you won't love me, I will love myself. I no longer need you, nor anyone. I will not be prisoner of myself, but master of myself. I will become a citadel against others. I will be my own God.

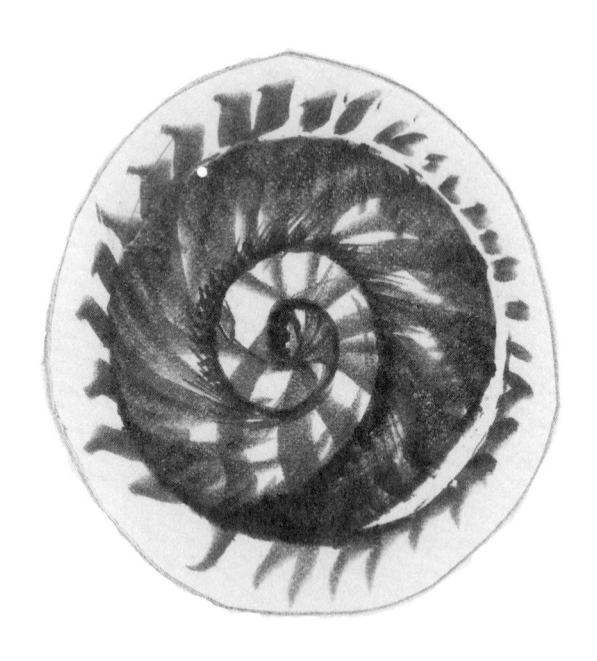

The Wrath of God

Death
I am secure now. I understand everything that happened to you and me. It is all perfectly clear. I see who was right and who was wrong.

The Institution
And I know what is right and wrong for others, too.

The Wrath of God
But I have no friends . . .

Hell
People can't hear me even when I scream at them . . .

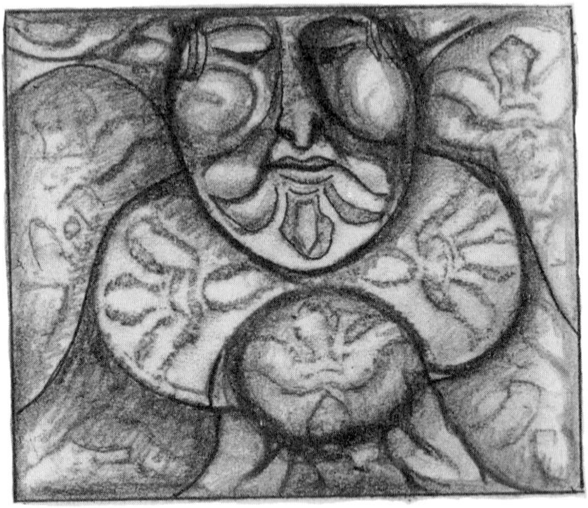

Despair

Maybe I don't know anything. But if that is true, what hope is there for me? I am desolate. Even death doesn't seem to be an answer, although I am no longer afraid to die. To be afraid is to feel something, and I am not aware of feeling anything. I am suspended from life, and I cannot die because I am not living. I am a stone.

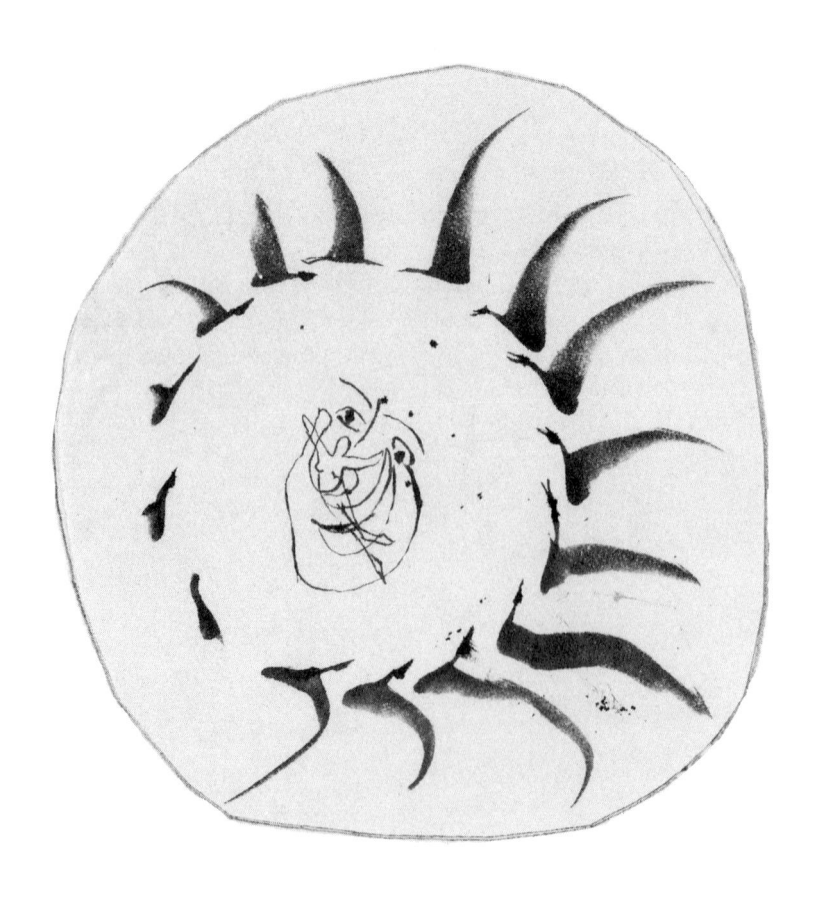

Miracle

Repentance

Help me. Can stones cry out? I thought I could be God, but I hear myself crying for help in a new voice, faint and weak. Can it be mine? I am too exhausted to care. I see that I am quite different from what I thought, and probably not worth paying attention to anyhow.

Miracle

Someone heard me . . .

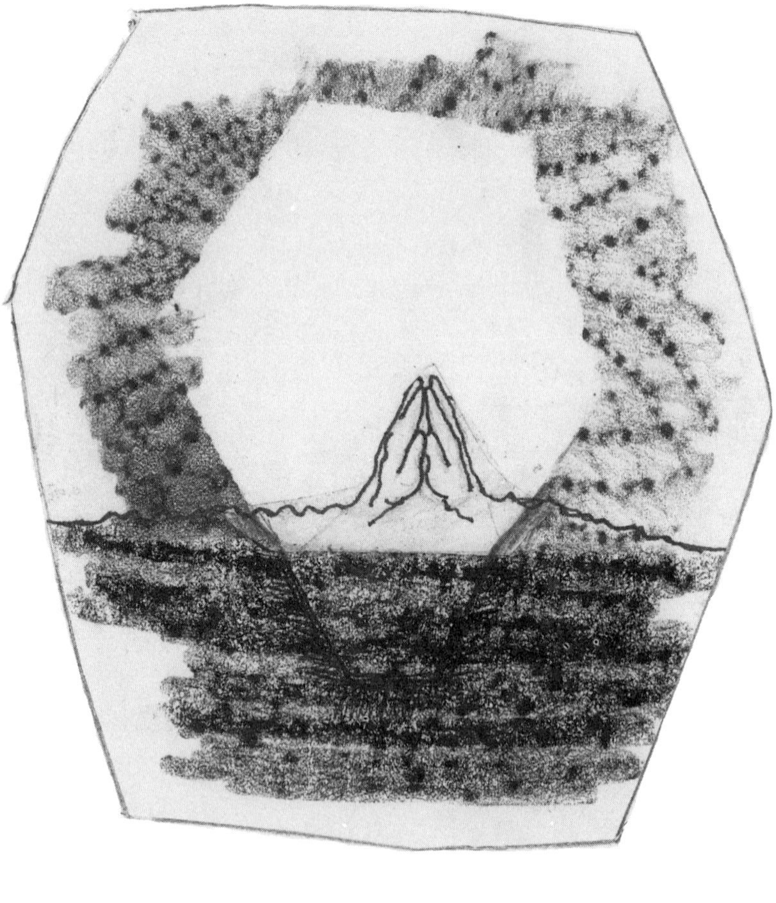

Forgiveness

My idea that life is a matter of you and me together is falling apart, and I am terrified. It is a fearful event, like a great iceberg exploding and crashing into the water. Perhaps the iceberg finds new life in the water that had been sustaining it even as an iceberg. Do you think life is like water, forgiving us, at its deepest level, for freezing ourselves into icebergs?

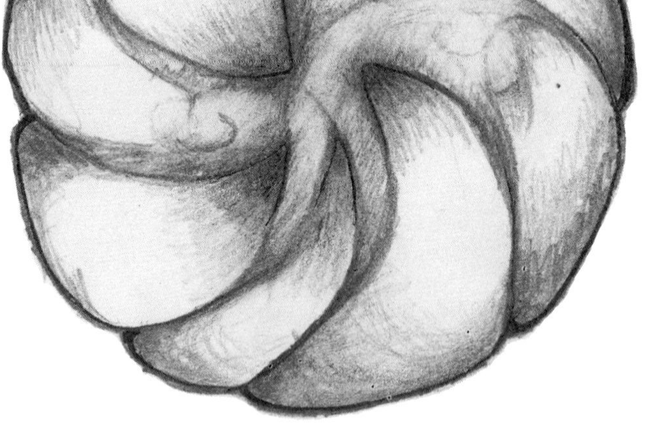

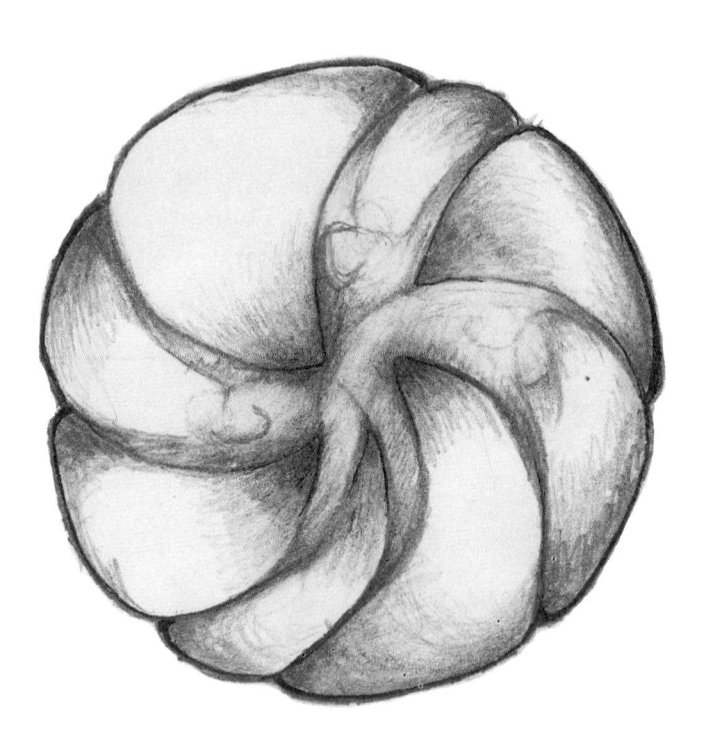

History

I've been thinking about us. I've come to see that I will never know what really happened. I can't seem to isolate "you" or "me," nor can I isolate the events of our story. Why do I try? Some things certainly seem to have happened in the past, but in a mysterious way they are still going on because the past is continually changing. Time is all mixed up, and the past is being unfolded by the future, now, in me.

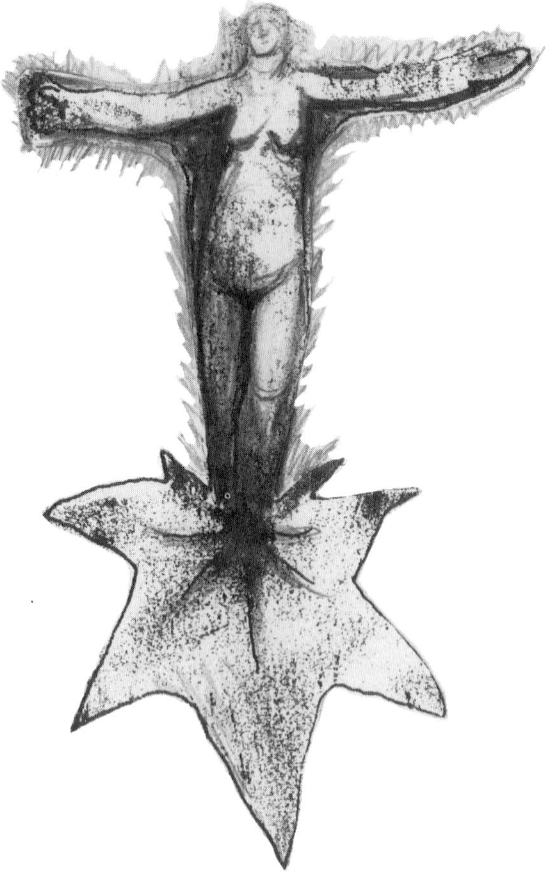

Creation

How could God have created me a long time ago? I am only just beginning to be. I am not a finished product, but a coming event. I am coming forth. But from what, from where? I am emerging out of all the events of the world, out of their relationship. Is relationship God?

Sin

Sin

If relationship is God, then I denied God when I denied you by not hearing you.

Love

Why did I think I loved you? I couldn't even hear you as a free person. It would have been better to have listened to you.

Incarnation

I see that it is by relationship that we are changed from things into persons. This must be the mystery of God, that relationship can be other than itself. Relationship is between, but it is given for us.

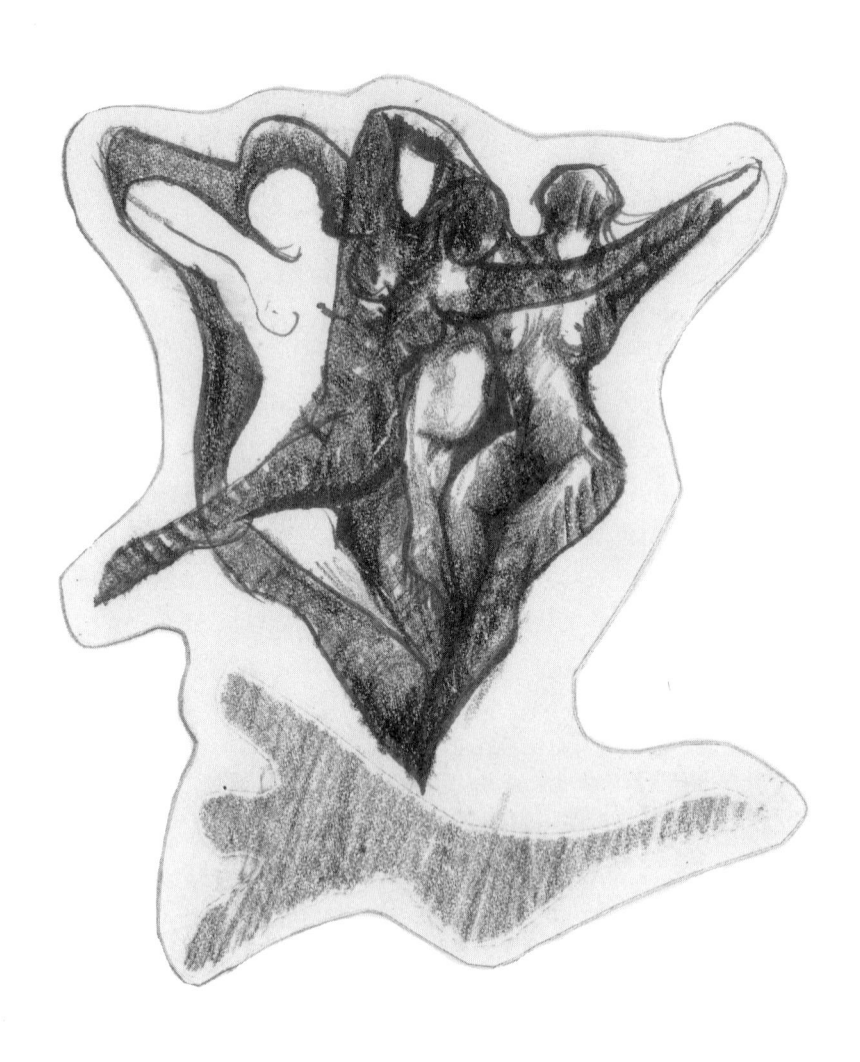

The Cross

The Cross

It seems we have a power to remain outside relationship, to be as a dead thing, rather than to become a living person. The power of relationship to create us as persons, and our power to remain as things, cross in the center of our lives. Where one power dies, the other is born.

The Empty Tomb

I see that I've been trying to solve the riddle of you by fixing you in my mind as a certain kind of person, but I haven't been able to do it. Just when I think I have finished with you, you disappear, and I can't say "There, that is the end of that." You remain a mystery.

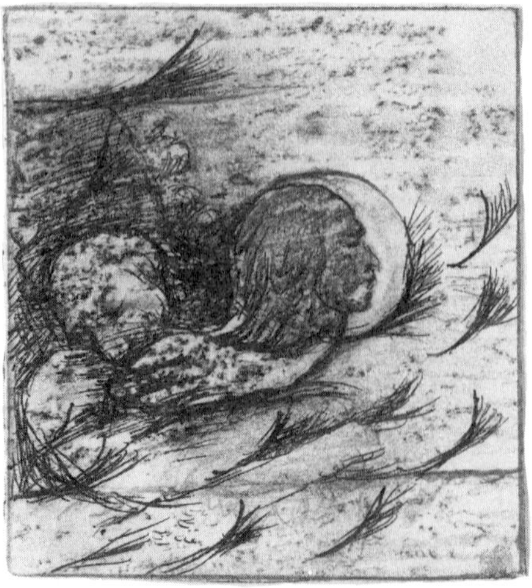

Resurrection

I am beginning to see you in a different light. Even though you are not with me anymore, you are becoming a new person to me. And I see myself anew, too.

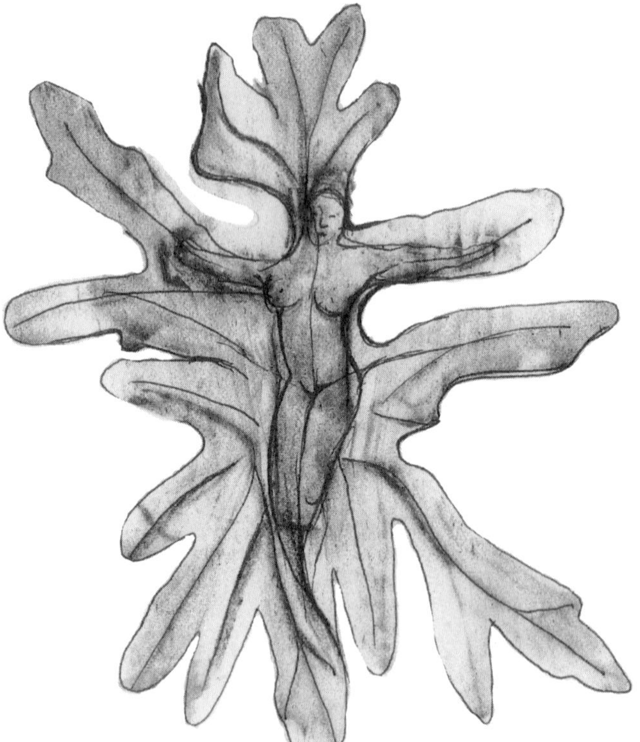

Faith

The new me hasn't lasted. But once in a while, here and there, I say something to someone or someone says something to me, and I feel it's happening again. It seems we never really *are*, are we? I mean not by ourselves. I am because you are, or because everyone is. But this "I" is always a new event, a happening. Am I a verb rather than a noun? A doing instead of a being? It comforts me to see that I could never really lose you, because "I" could never really have "you."

And sitteth on the right hand of God the Father

Ascension into Heaven

You were most present to me when I finally realized I could never know you.

And sitteth on the right hand of God the Father

Now you have your own freedom, from me . . .

The Holy Spirit

I see that I will never really understand everything. The power of relationship is such that it works without our knowing it. In fact, if we try to force it, it goes away. I think that is what happened to you. I didn't trust the relationship between us.

Eternal Life

Eternal Life

I am letting go of my idea of time. I see that eternal life is not a question of "I will be forever," but of "Now I am." Eternity is time dying in me.

Losing One's Self

And so it seems that there is no point in struggling to find my "self," in the sense of reaching a final goal. Why? Because just as there is no place where I can stop and say "There, that was you," so there is no place where I can stop and say "Here, this is me." To say *I am* is not the same as saying *This is me*. One is eternal life; the other, death.

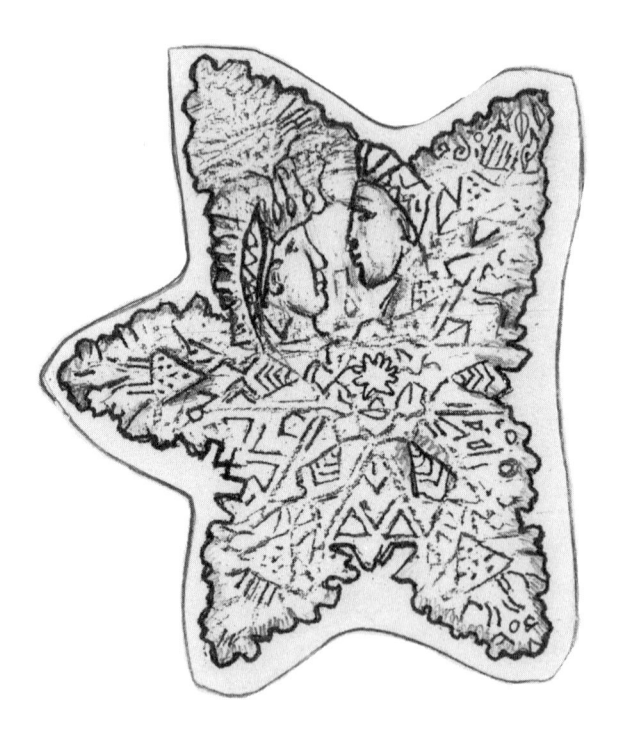

The Great Commandment

The Good News

This task of becoming persons, therefore, is not something we have to do by ourselves. It is done for us, by the power of relationship to create us as persons.

The Great Commandment

Therefore, listen to one another . . .

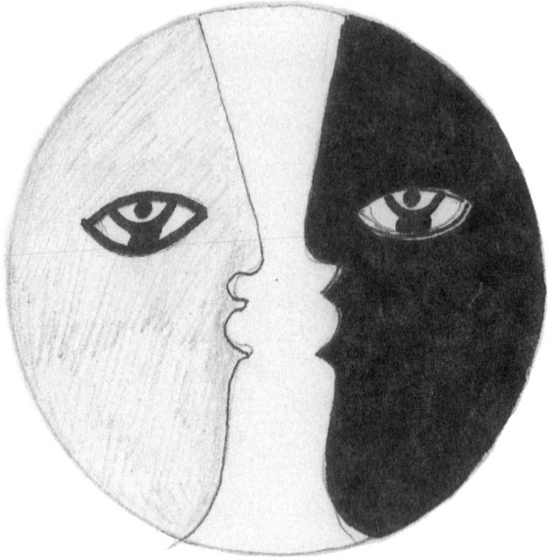

Prayer

. . . for each of us speaks as a cry to God. Each of us is a prayer for the overcoming of the death that is in us. Each of us is a prayer for a new way to be.

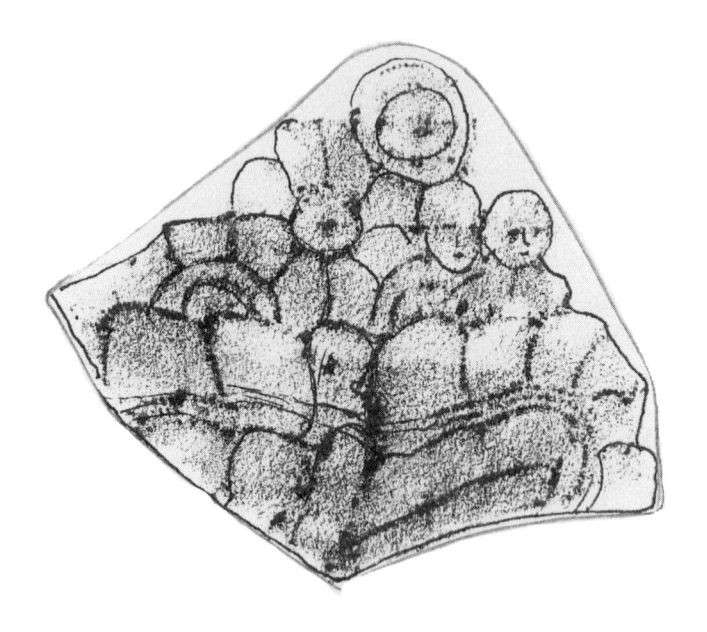

Religion

The Church

The possibility of new relationship is hidden in the heart of life. This is the "church" that is neither in a place, nor in a person, but between persons. We must look for it everywhere.

Religion

I think you and I were wrong to worship God as we did. We had to stop paying attention to others to do it. Such worship separates, just as my worshiping you separated me from you. I think it is better to love God than to worship God, for this kind of separation can only be overcome by Love.

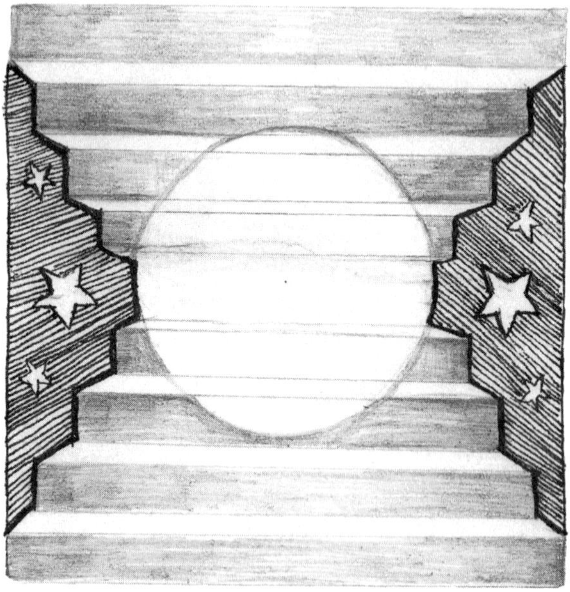

Sacraments

But this does not mean we should do away with sacraments. On the contrary, we should try to see them everywhere. To celebrate what is, is a sacrament. We do not create sacraments, they create us.

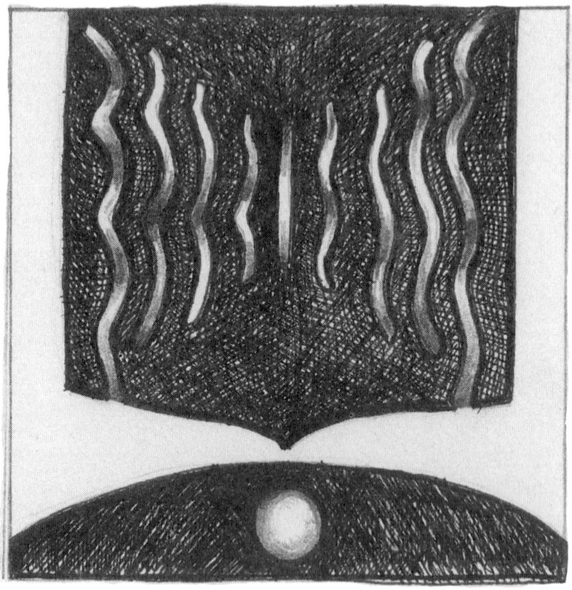

Marriage

Marriage is a commitment to discovery, a celebration of the sacrament of relationship. When we stop discovering each other anew, we cease becoming persons for each other, and the marriage is ended. To pretend there is a marriage when in fact there isn't one, is to create a tomb in the midst of life. "What God hath joined together, let no one put asunder," but what God hath not kept together, let no one hold imprisoned."

Divorce

Divorce

Divorce is the loss of the ability to find something new in each other. Divorce is how we know God can die.

Re-Marriage

Although God can die, God can live again, in a new way.

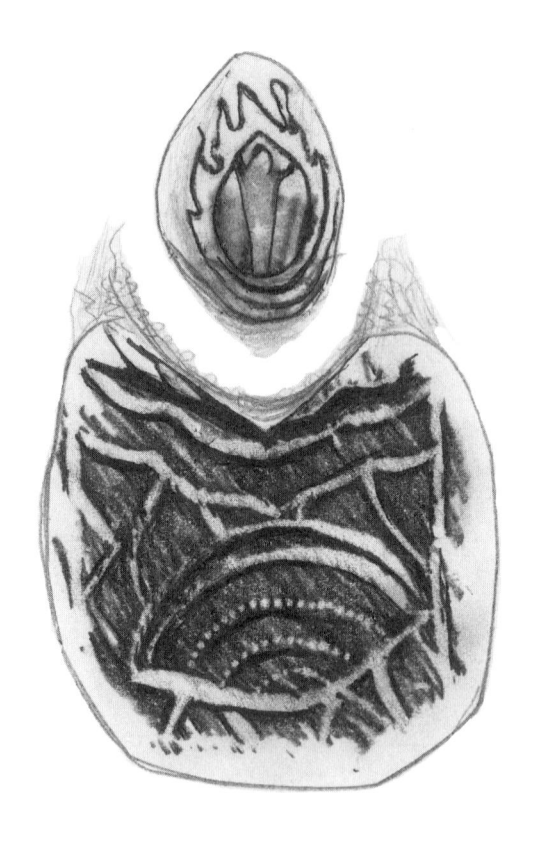

Life

The New Family

Those who offer us new life are our true parents, and those to whom we offer new life, our children.

Life

Life is not just a matter of eating, breathing, and sleeping, but a fire warming the world. This is why when someone dies, we feel a chill.

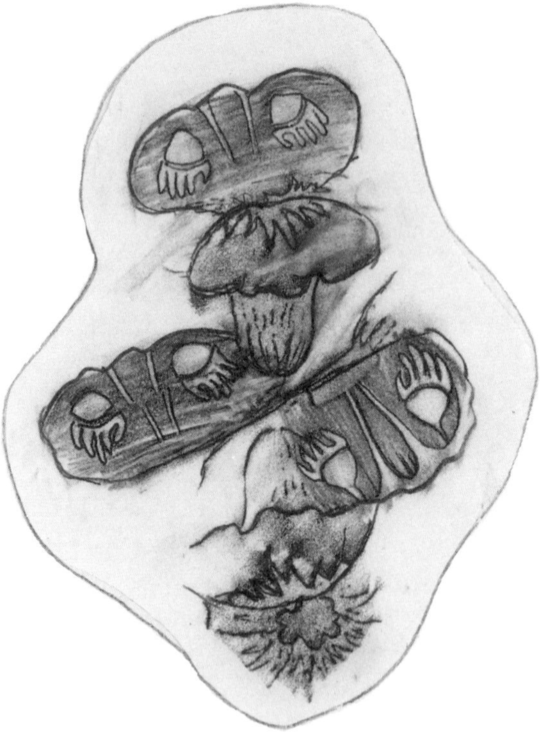

The Second Coming

In the beginning everything was in relationship, and in the end everything will be in relationship again. In the meantime, we live by hope.

Revelation

And, finally, I see that what I thought was a curse turned out to be a blessing. For we wouldn't have had a story at all if I hadn't tried to find out the name of it.

THE AWAKENING OF ADAM

And the Lord placed Adam in the garden to tend and care for it.
Genesis

To die and be re-born is not easy.
Fritz Perls

Introduction

How is it that I, a woman, presume to write about Adam, a man? I think it is because Adam lives in each of us, just as Eve does. I haven't always known this. I was led to reflecting on Adam at a time when I wanted so much to understand a man I loved. What did he feel? What did he want? How did he experience our relationship?

I put myself in Adam's heart, as Eve, and discovered that life was more mysterious than I had imagined. I came to realize that there was an Adam in me, and probably in everyone.

And who is Adam? He is the one who thinks he understands how life works. When God tells him to till the soil and tend the garden, he goes straight to work, believing that God has nothing more to say to him. When Eve appears in his life, he finds that something more is required.

What happens after that is a story of growing up.

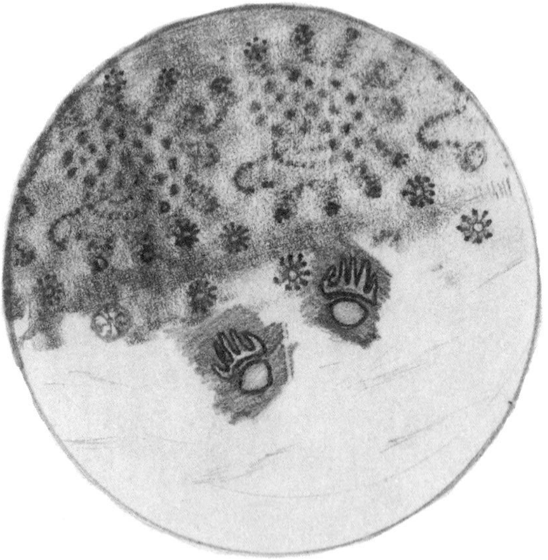

The Beginning

In the beginning I enjoyed working at the tasks given to me. I had no awareness then of suffering or pain, either in myself or in the life around me. I did not think of the past or spend time worrying about the future. I lived in the moment, without fear.

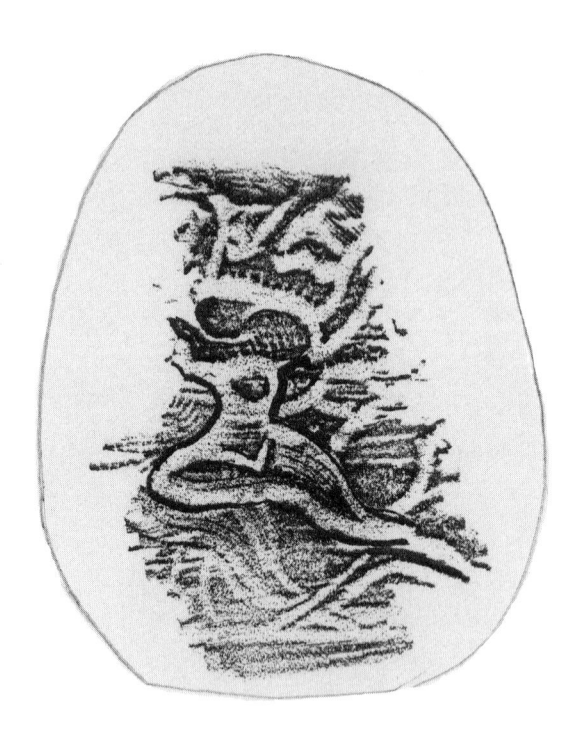

Separation

Desire
I thought it would be a pleasure to share myself with someone.

Separation
That other was *you.*

Temptation
I wanted to make you a part of me.

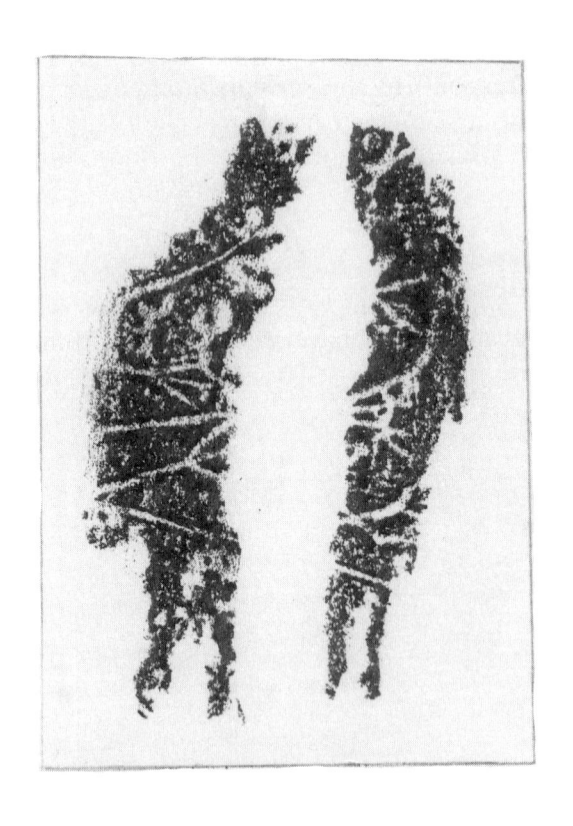

Expulsion from the Garden

The Fall

Because I thought you would give me a new kind of freedom.

Punishment

But why do I feel trapped? I think it is because you are always clinging to me with your talk of love.

Expulsion from the Garden

I am living like a prisoner. There is nothing to do but work and try to find my freedom again.

Idolatry

Idolatry

My work gives me a sense of power, and I am willing to sacrifice everything for it.

The Institution

I can show people how to be as successful as I am, but they have to do it my way.

Evil

Murder

But there is always someone who threatens me. I must destroy him.

Evil

Now I am the center of the universe.

The Wrath of God

And yet I feel so alone. Why is there no one with me?

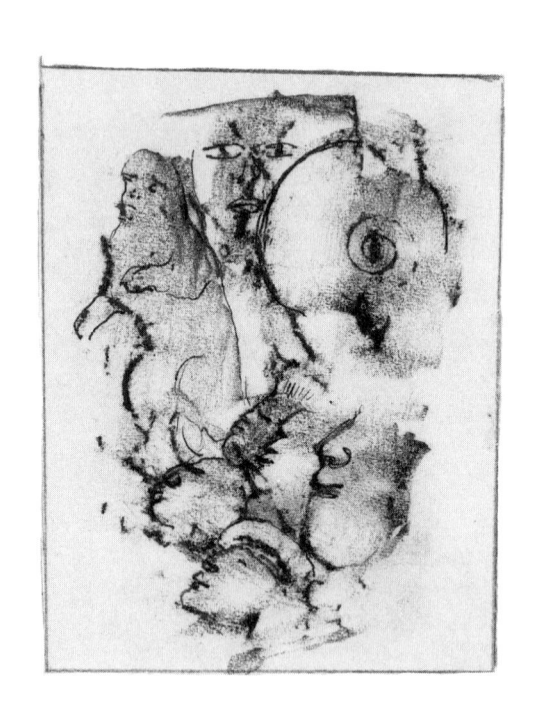

Hell

Death
I keep my true feelings hidden from everyone, even from myself.

Hell
And I no longer know who or what I am.

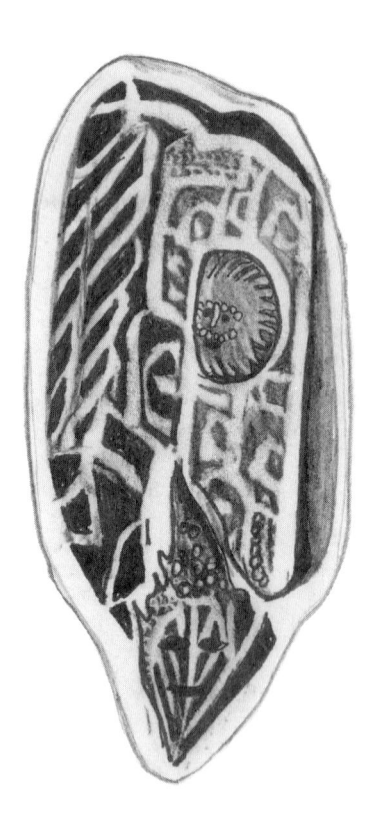

Despair

Despair

Where am I? There is no one out there to answer me, and I am afraid. I am more than afraid; I am lost. Where is my power, my strength?

Repentance

It seems I am not as invulnerable as I thought. I need someone. I need a you.

Miracle

Miracle

You came back, but as a different person.

Forgiveness

We can talk to each other now.

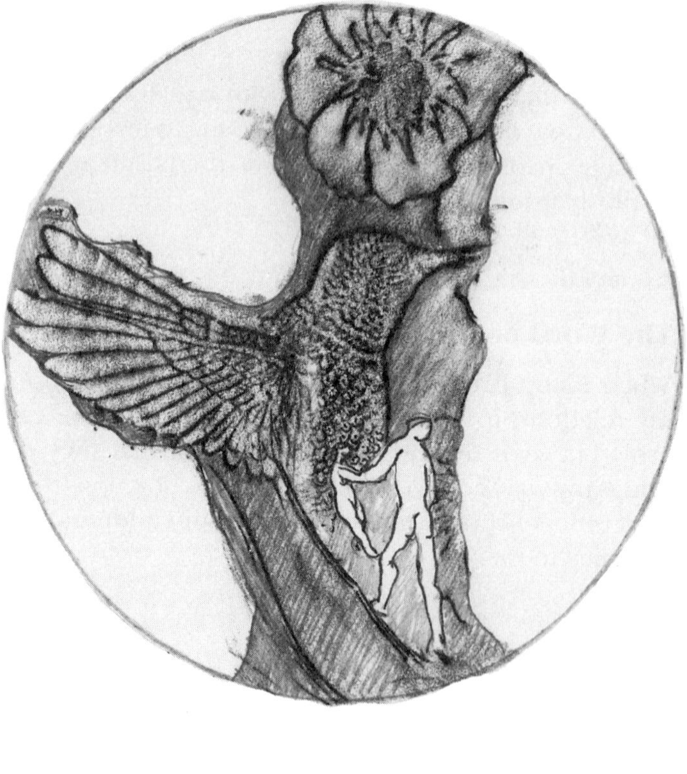

New Life

I see that you are different because you have chosen me out of your own freedom. I can love you now in a new and better way. I do not need you to be an extension of me, but only to be you. I find you full of surprises and that is delightful.

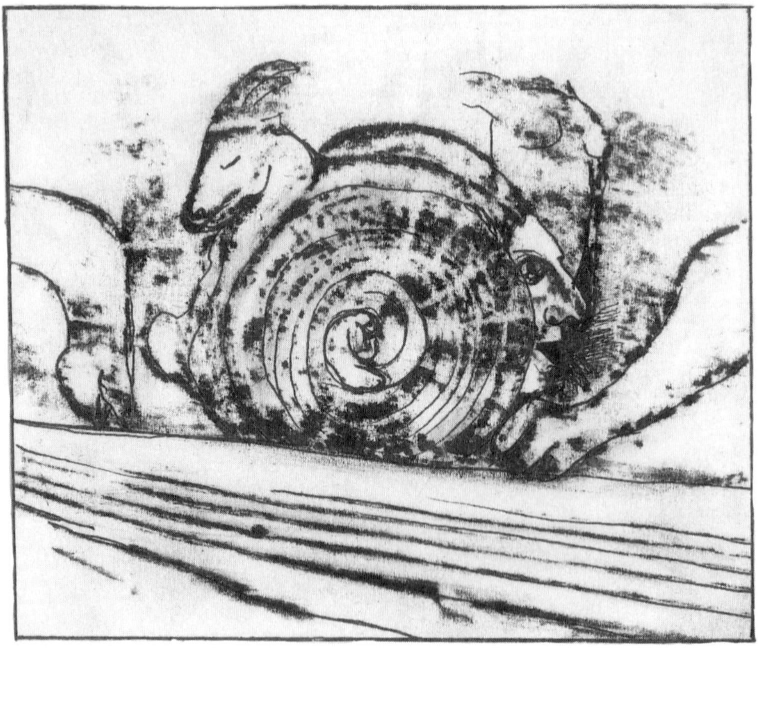

History

I am astonished to discover that we have a common history. You were struggling to find your freedom as much as I, and I see that we each had to find it in ourselves. Your talk of "love" frightened me as much as my talk of "freedom" frightened you. I felt you were a trap, and you felt I was a threat. Our life together might fall into this danger once again if we do not remember our free choice.

Sacrifice

Sacrifice

I see that love must give itself to freedom because love is the greater power. But freedom must remember love's gift, to keep from becoming destructive.

Incarnation

I think love gives us our freedom in order that we might give freedom to our love.

Freedom

Freedom

Why do I speak so much about freedom? I think it is because I am beginning to realize that it is not something we work toward, but something we have right now. If we do not have it right now, then we never will have it. Our freedom is our freedom to say "I," and this is not something that someone else gives us, but something we choose or do not choose. I was wrong to expect you to give me my freedom. You can only give me your own.

Responsibility

I see that I must be aware of how my freedom affects others, and take responsibility for the way I use my freedom.

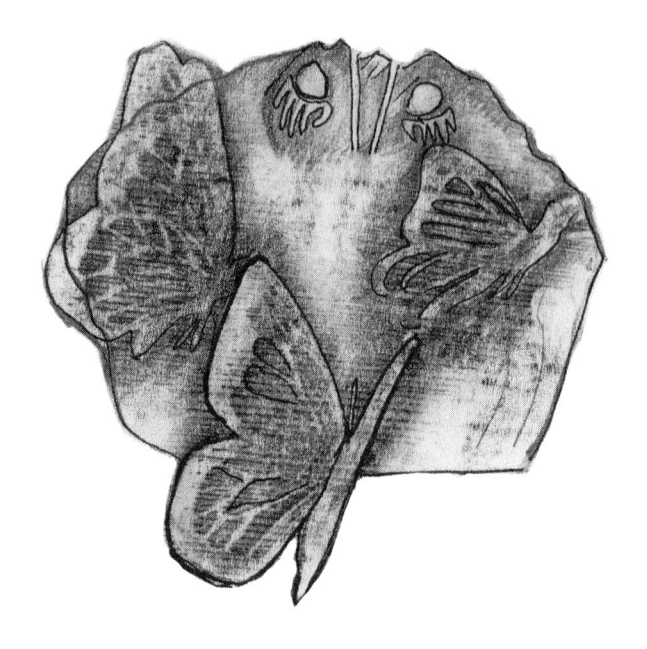

Atonement

Destiny

And when I use my freedom to choose, I know that my freedom is limited by the result of my choice.

Atonement

I am becoming aware of how indebted I am to the choices others have made before me, and how my life exists because of the price others have paid for it.

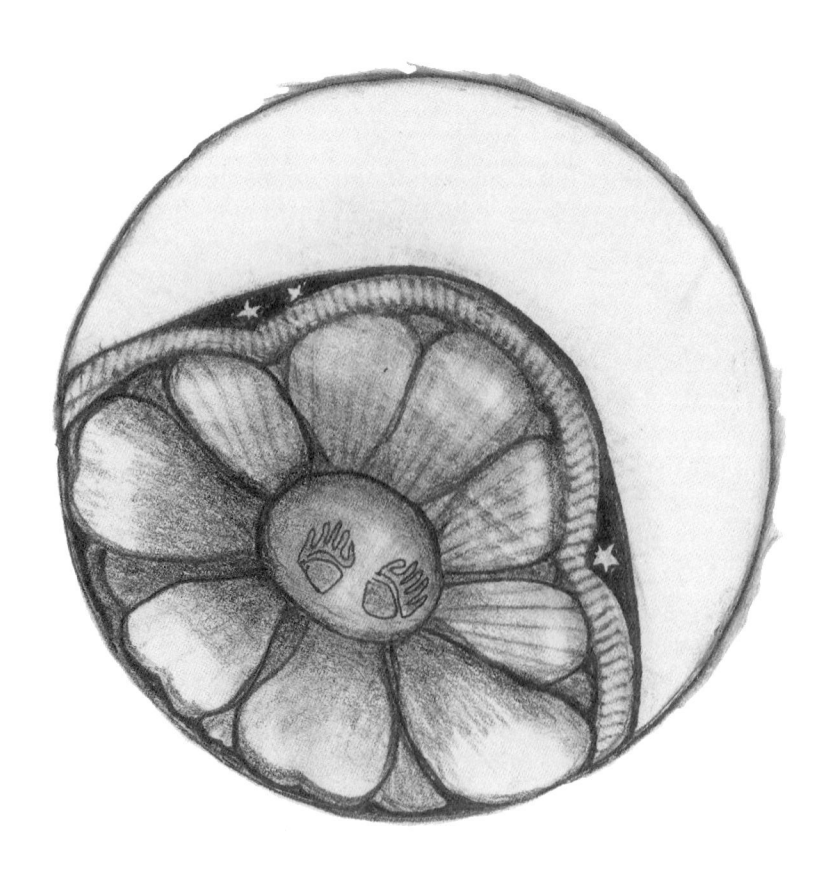

Salvation

The Communion of Saints

I am part of a network of events that have occurred in the lives of many people, some of whom are unknown to me. I know that their deaths must have contributed to my life, and that without them I would not be who I am. To be aware of this is to carry their love within my heart, and to live in a spirit of gratitude.

Salvation

And now as I take responsibility for myself, without losing the awareness of my debt to life, I feel I have come home to myself.

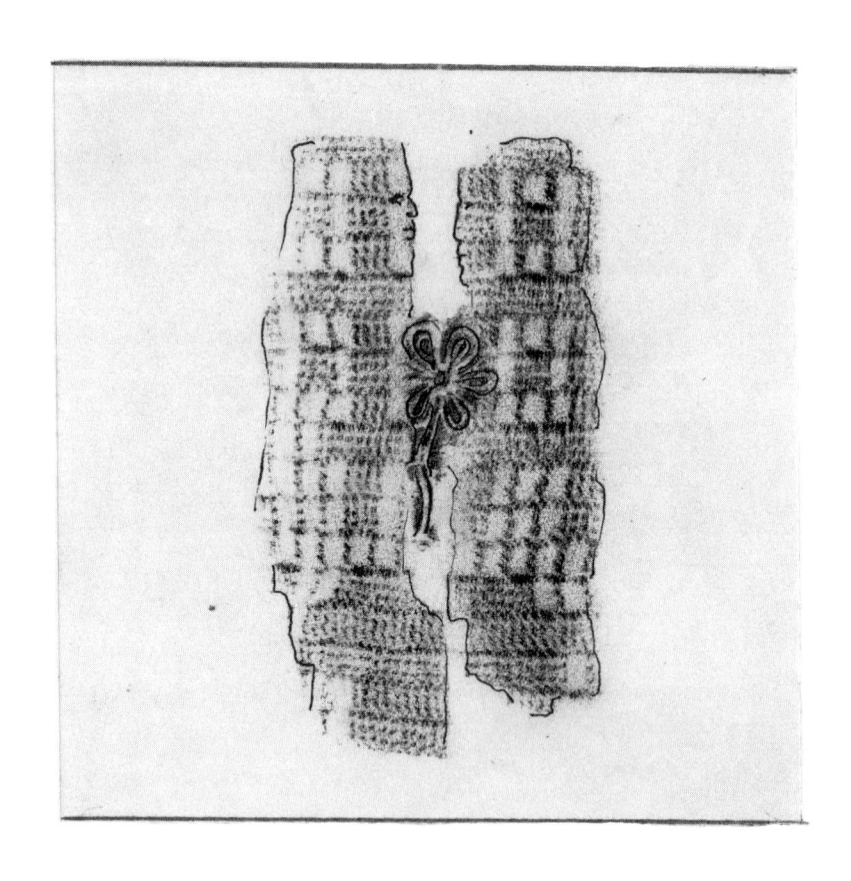

The Word of Life

The Good News

I see now that all change begins with myself, and when I admit how difficult that is, I stop trying to force others to make up for my deficiencies. I find this is a great relief to those around me.

The Word of Life

When I stop blaming others for my present situation, my relationship with them vastly improves. Love can grow between us, for I do not demand that they do things my way, nor do I feel that I have to do things their way, unless I choose to. I can talk to our children now, and they to me.

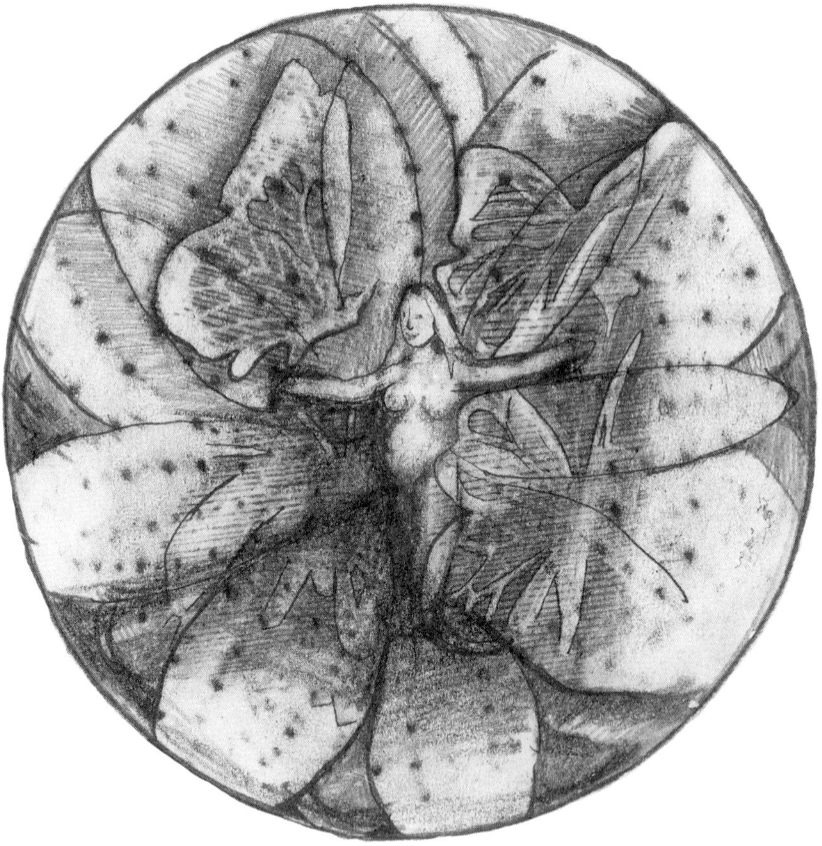

Life

I know now that the life of a man is not just a matter of being born, living and dying, but a process of becoming human. There is something beyond nature in this "humanness" of man, something that calls forth personal life out of the world of nature. I think this is what we call the *divine* in man, and we come to an awareness of it as we struggle to discover what it means to say "I."

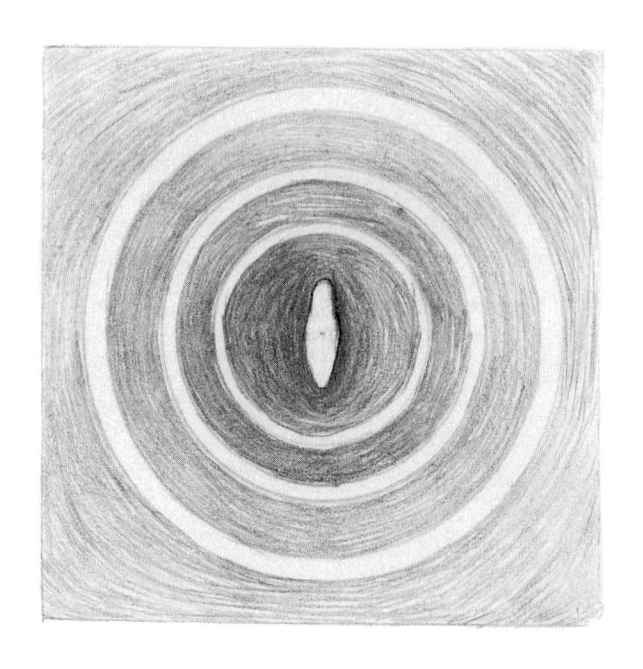

The Empty Tomb

The Empty Tomb

To be aware that a person has a deeper dimension in her life that can never be fully visible, is to know that she cannot be analyzed and filed away like an object. I can only know you by loving you, not by analyzing you. You will always escape my analysis of you and remain, essentially, a mystery.

Hope

And when we look into each other's eyes, we give each other a gift from the world of our invisible *I,* and in that world we are one, and all is known and all forgiven.

Divorce

Marriage

I feel our life together is indissoluble now because we truly care for each other's freedom and growth.

Divorce

If we stop caring for each other's growth life divorces us.

Eternal Life

Eternal Life

To respond to the present moment in life is to live without blame or fear, and when I do this, I feel in touch with something in me that is beyond time.

Redemption

I feel as though I have recovered something I lost long ago.

Creation

Work

And I am enjoying my work once more. I know now that work can't give me my freedom, but I can bring my freedom to my work.

Creation

Work is such a habit with me that I cannot cease making things. But can I ever make something as mysterious and complicated as myself? I seem to be creating myself as I grow, and yet I am always beyond myself and before myself. Who and what shall I be in the end? And how did I begin this journey? Who set me on this path?

Faith

God

There is a power that enables me to become more real to myself when I take responsibility for my freedom. If this power is God, then God's other name must be Love, because the more real I become to myself, the more I can love others.

Faith

And how can I prove that *God* is *Love?* I can't; I can only know it by what has happened in my life.

Resurrection

It is curious that the more I am aware of people, the more complex and beautiful they become, until at times I find myself in awe of a stranger standing before me. I do not know her, and yet she appears familiar, and when she looks into my eyes, I feel she knows me better than I know myself.

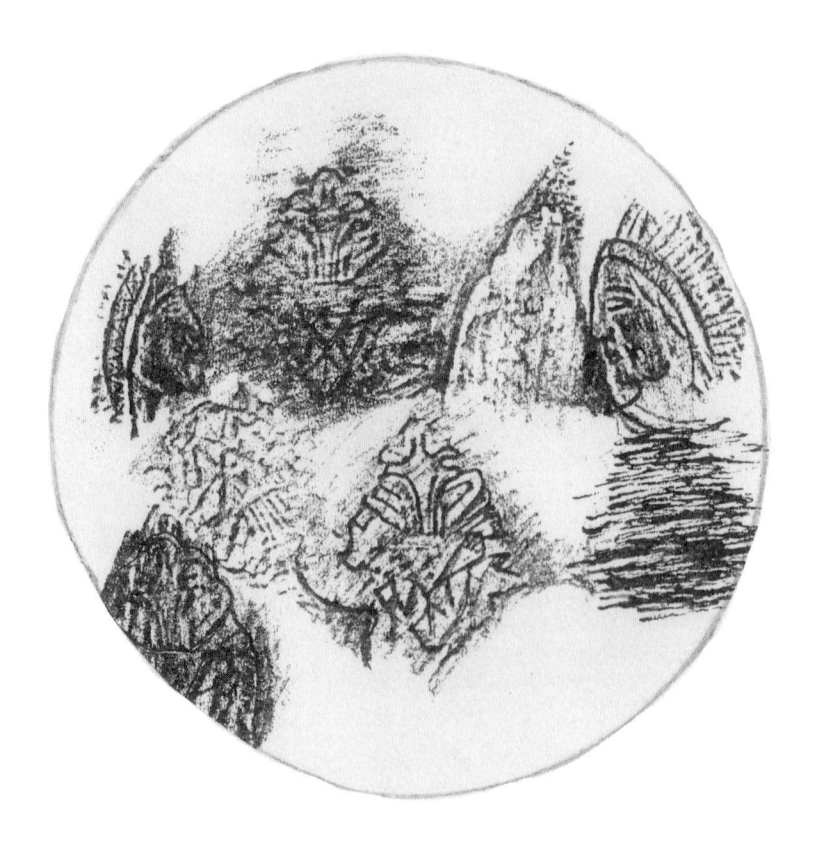

The Church

The Great Commandment

Therefore we must have reverence for each other and let each other grow, for each of us manifests the prayer of our true "I" to be born in us and become visible to the other.

The Church

There are times when I feel the need to join with others as we share our awareness of the mystery of our freedom.

Sin

Somewhere deep inside myself I know I sinned when I let my life become mechanical, when I did not let myself see other people as persons, with their own freedom.

Grace

Grace

I am grateful that my life is not just an isolated fact, but an event that emerges out of the life around me, which gives me support in ways that I do not always deserve.

Revelation

I thought my story was to be one of pleasure but it turned out to be full of suffering. But in the suffering I see the birth of love, and the birth of love was the birth of the man.

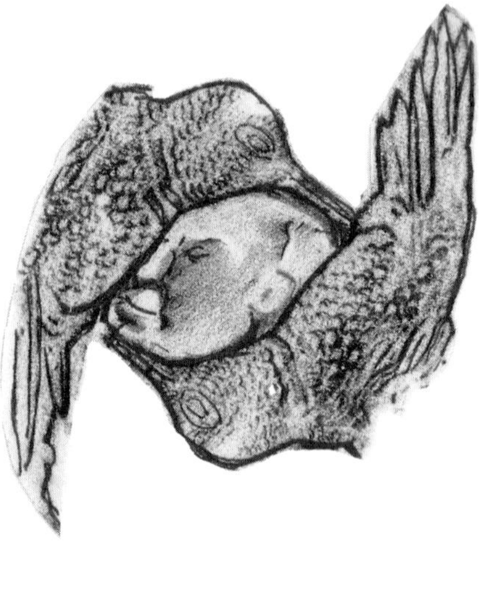

The New Man

I see that the truth of my life is not, finally, something I know, but *someone I am,* the one I may never know until my death.

THE LIBERATION OF ISAAC AND ABRAHAM

After these things God tested Abraham, and said to him, "Abraham," and he said, "Here I am." He said, "Take your son, your only son Isaac, whom you love, and go to the mountain of Moriah and offer him there as a burnt offering upon one of the mountains of which I shall tell you."
Genesis

Little by little, wean yourself.
Rumi

Introduction

Not everyone has been, or is, a parent. Everyone has been a child. As children, we long to grow up and feel free, and this involves suffering, both for ourselves and our parents.

This is a story about that suffering. It begins in captivity and ends in freedom. It is about possessive love, which can destroy another.

I was prompted to reflect on Isaac and Abraham as I witnessed my children's journey through life with me as their parent. I saw how their freedom was inseparable from my own. I thought a lot about parents and children, and what happens between them. What is our duty? And how is that related to love?

It must have been a long, hard walk up that mountain before Isaac and Abraham found their freedom together. I imagine that Abraham felt a fierce tension in him between wanting to hold on and knowing he must let go. I like to think he experienced Eve and Adam coming to life in him, as him. Like them, he is rescued by love. It is that love which finally sets Isaac and Abraham free.

This well-known story has been mined for its meaning by many scholars far more qualified than I. They have used the tools of language, history, tradition, and psychological insight to probe its depth.

It is said about this story that Abraham's "faith" was tested. Faith means more than belief. It means something like trusting with the heart, and I think that is what happened to Abraham. He began to trust with his heart. Therefore, the story of Abraham and Isaac is, for me, a love story.

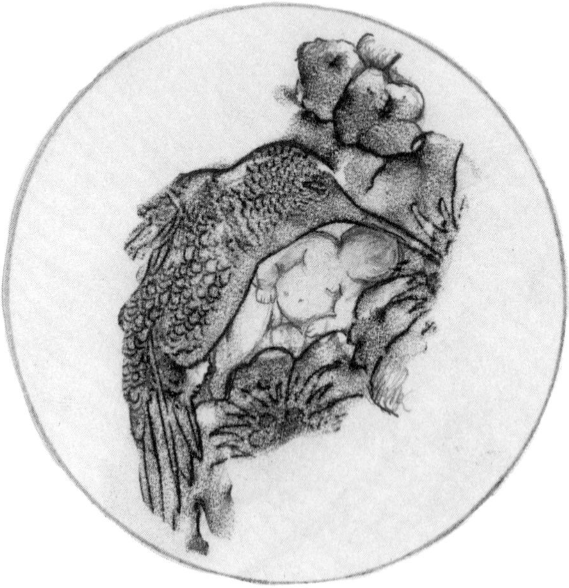

The Beginning

Your arrival was the greatest joy of my life. I could scarcely believe the surprise of you, my own child. I praised God that you had been sent to me.

Promise

Promise
Through you I believed I would realize the meaning of my life.

Desire
I longed for you to have the same experience of happiness in your life.

Temptation
And I felt it was my duty to teach you how to live.

The Fall

The Fall
Therefore I made you the center of my existence . . .

Punishment
. . . and you obeyed me, but without heart.

Expulsion from the Garden
I feel that my love for you places many demands on me, and that your way of life is becoming a threat to me.

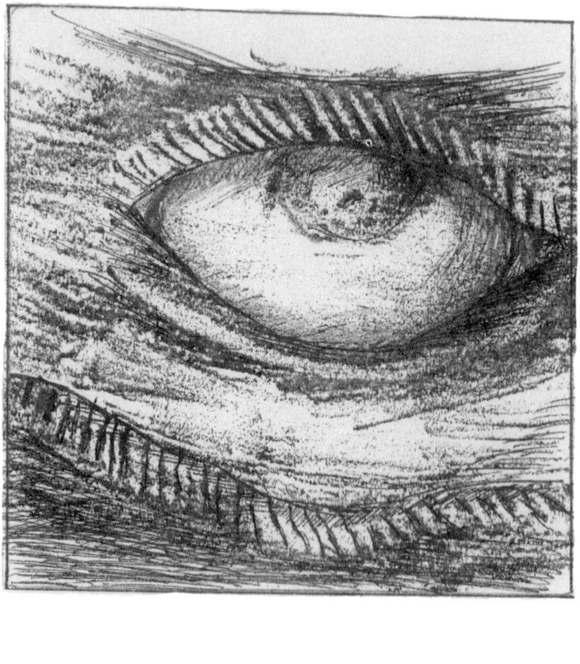

Idolatry
I make·more and more sacrifices for you . . .

Expectation
. . . but you seem blind to what I do for you.

Preparation
I resent your turning away from me, toward others.

The Test

The Test

I know better than you what you should do with your life. I love you more than you appreciate.

Obedience

And I shall fulfill my responsibilities toward you even if I have to isolate you from everyone . . .

Propitiation

. . . because I believe your future depends on me.

Hell

Murder

Therefore, you must live up to my expectations.

Hell

Somehow my love for you has become my need of you. And my need has driven you further from me. Now you and I are alone in our battle for existence. Which one of us shall survive?

The Grace of God

The Grace of God

I feel you are no longer a part of me. You are escaping me, and I do not know how to reach you.

Despair

All that you meant to me as promise and fulfillment for my life is lost. And I am lost. I can do nothing further with you.

Sacrifice

Sacrifice

I love you too much to watch you being destroyed by that very love. I give up my claim on your life.

Love

You are free now.

Miracle

I have seen you begin to be your real self again. How has it happened?

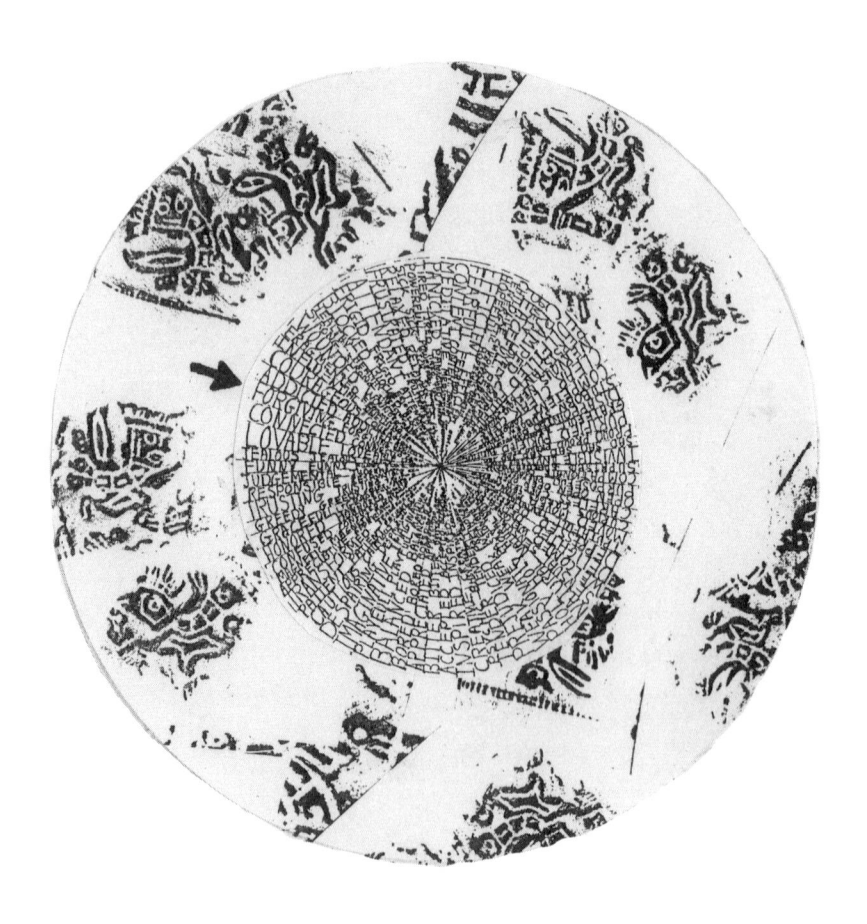

Forgiveness

The Good News

By giving up my claim on you I have discovered a new kind of love for you . . .

Forgiveness

. . . and you come to me now of your own accord.

Faith

I am grateful that I no longer resent your listening to others . . .

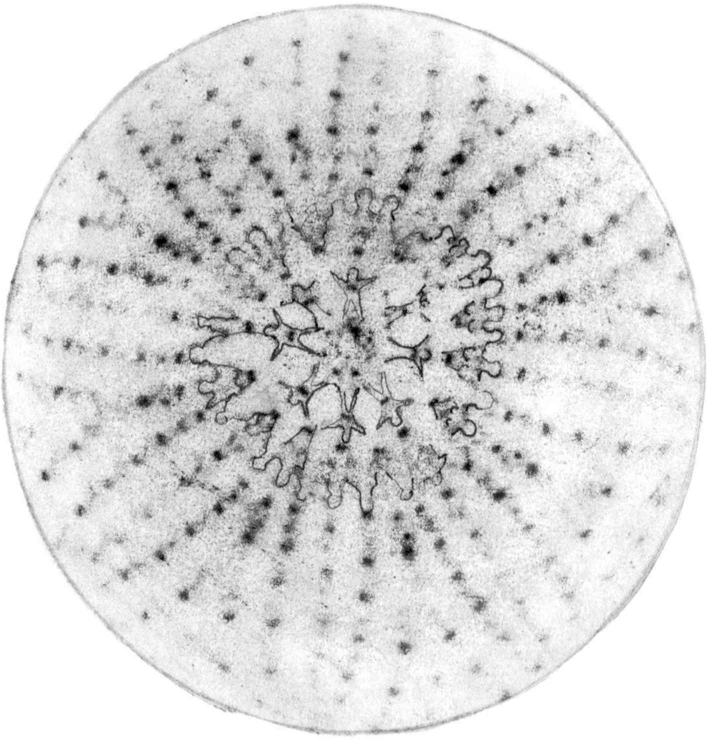

New Life

. . . and in an unexpected way, my own life has become fuller. I find my family is larger than I thought, because now I can love other people's children as well as my own. I have become a parent to many, to my great surprise.*

*Because you have done this, and not withheld your son, your only son, I will indeed bless you and I will multiply your descendants as the stars in heaven, and as the sand which is on the seashore.
Genesis

Death

Sin

It is not easy for me to see how my love became destructive, but I think it was when I believed you belonged to me alone.

Death

Because I can see now that my possession of you was leading to the death of life in you.

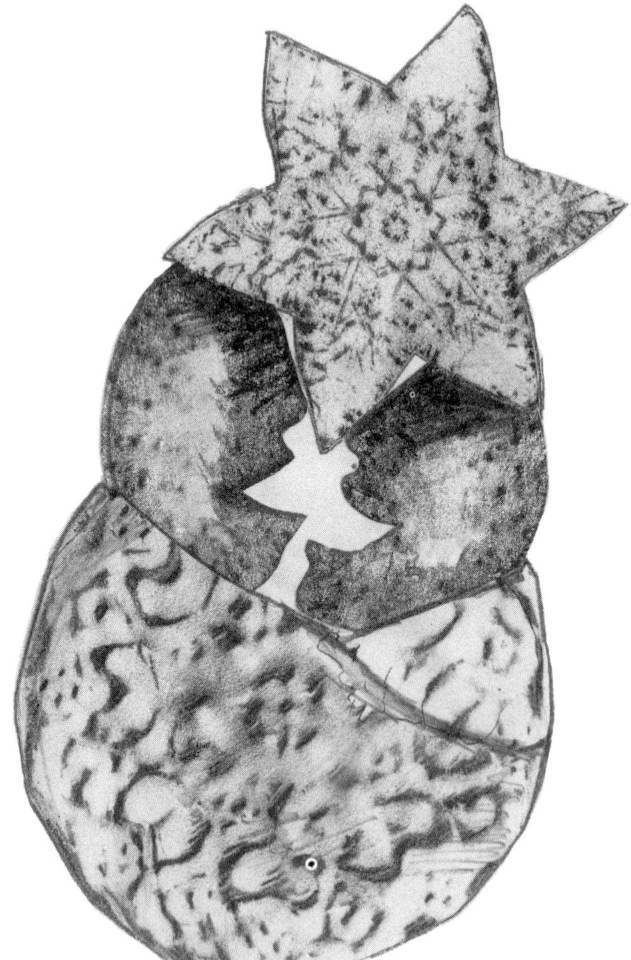

Resurrection

But now I can rejoice that your life is becoming rich with people and experience. When we meet there is much to talk about and the greatest joy is when we laugh together.*

*The root of the Hebrew name "Isaac" is *sahaq*, "to laugh."

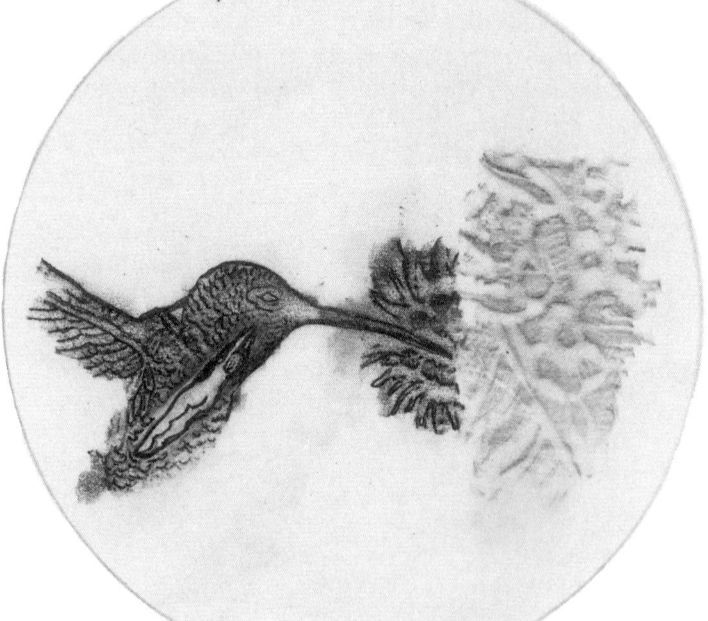

Revelation

And, finally, I see that the promise you held for me has been fulfilled, but not in the way that I expected. Now I live in gratitude for this astonishing mystery.

I tell you I have a long way to go before I am—where one begins.
Rainer Maria Rilke

Before Abraham was, I am.
Jesus

ABOUT THE AUTHOR

Jean Lanier, who is seventy, has pursued three questions in her life: What is love? What is life? What is God? The pondering of these questions has led her to the acceptance of life as Mystery. She married into a leading banking family, and after the death of her first husband took up the study of theology and subsequently of psychotherapy.

For the past twenty-four years she has been married to Sidney Lanier, with whom she co-founded a residential center for human potential in Spain. She has six children and six grandchildren.

Jean Lanier works as a spiritually oriented therapist in San Francisco and contributes a regular column to Matthew Fox's *Creation* magazine. Her publications include a book of poetry entitled *Diagnoses and Other Poems*.

ABOUT THE ARTIST

California artist Marion Weber studied art at the Museum School of Fine Arts in Boston and drawing with Nerina Sime in Florence, Italy. She is well known for her exquisite tapestries in which she uses a pointillist technique of her own invention. She runs the Healing Arts Center in Stinson Beach, California.